THE HITCHHIKER'S GUIDE TO
Finding and Preparing for a New Job

THE HITCHHIKER'S GUIDE TO
Finding and Preparing for a New Job

By Cecilia A. Haberzettl, PhD

AACC Press
2101 L Street, NW, Suite 202
Washington, DC 20037-1526
www.aacc.org

© 1999, American Association for Clinical Chemistry, Inc. All rights reserved. No part of this publication may be reproduced, stored in a retrieval system, or transmitted in any form by electronic, mechanical, photocopying, or any other means without permission of the publisher.

1-890883-19-0

Printed in the USA

ABOUT THE AUTHOR

Over the last 25 years, Cecilia A. Haberzettl, PhD, has held 13 different positions—nine as the result of promotions within the same organization—in eight different organizations: Union Carbide, Warner Lambert Research Institute, Fairleigh Dickinson University, St. Barnabas Medical Center, Sandoz, Inc., Johnson & Johnson, UMDNJ-Robert Wood Johnson Medical School, and Centocor, Inc.

Her first experience with downsizing was back in the 1970's, when the words "severance" and "outplacement" were uncommon. Following Centocor's divestiture of its diagnostics business, Dr. Haberzettl worked with three outplacement organizations and two personal outplacement counselors. Today she is president of C. A. Haberzettl and Associates, an organization that provides consulting services related to laboratory medicine. There she brings a clinical perspective to the early stages of diagnostic product development and leverages the synergies between laboratory medicine and therapeutics.

Dr. Haberzettl's career is characterized by progressive growth and contributions as scientist and director in clinical, diagnostic, and pharmaceutical/biotechnology settings. Her experience includes all aspects of product development, from concept to market introduction to product support. Additional experience in the areas of regulatory submissions (infectious diseases and oncology) and clinical trials (AIDS and cardiovascular) provides a well-rounded background in diagnostic laboratory medicine and clinical trials for therapeutics.

Broad yet in-depth and hands-on, her background is complemented by a strategic approach to gaining insights into the trends and key drivers in healthcare and laboratory medicine. This experience was primarily obtained through more than 12 years as an ex-officio or elected member of the Board of Directors of the American Association for Clinical Chemistry (AACC). This combination of hands-on and strategic experience gives Dr. Haberzettl a unique perspective on selecting and developing products for the field of laboratory medicine.

Dr. Haberzettl's formal education includes a degree in medical technology from Orange County Community College in Middletown, New York, and a doctorate in biomedical sciences from UMDNJ-Robert Wood Johnson Medical School/Rutgers University in New Brunswick, New Jersey.

ACKNOWLEDGEMENTS

During my transition period, I had the good fortune and pleasure of working with Mr. Ed Kelleher (Kelleher Associates, Wayne, PA) as one of my outplacement counselors. He went far beyond providing the "standard" outplacement support and I count Ed among my network of professional friends. A good listener, Ed provided advice specific to my background and needs. Providing such personalized coaching and sharing his wisdom and insights is characteristic of Ed's approach to career counseling.

As I describe in Chapter 7, I identified a "board of directors" whom I could go to for advice, encouragement, constructive criticism and to share my progress with. Their advice and long time support have been invaluable to me in my career and especially during my transition period. Two of my "board" members are former managers from our mutual time with J&J: Dr. Paul Kaplan, currently vice president of research at Affymetrix, and Dr. Jack Geltosky, currently vice president of scientific licensing and worldwide business development at SmithKline Beecham Pharmaceuticals. As I comment later, good managers are supportive long after you move onto new opportunities. My third "board" member is a long time AACC colleague, Dr. Sue Evans, currently vice president of research and development at Dade Behring Inc. Sue and I have shared many experiences on various AACC committees and most recently as elected members of AACC's Board of Directors.

During my time with Centocor, I participated in an individualized management coaching program with Benton Management Resources. Following that program, I sought and received feedback from several levels of senior management on my potential to move into the ranks of senior management. Mr. Dave Holveck, Centocor's chief executive officer, evolved into a mentor for me as a result of that initial contact. Dave has provided much helpful advice and shared his wisdom "from the CEO's side of the table" on such topics as taking charge of my career development, technology assessment, writing a résumé and preparing to interview with a CEO. I am gratified that Dave still finds time to share his insights long after the restructuring ended my employment with Centocor.

My transition process led me to an alternate (but related) career option as a consultant. Before making this decision, I discussed the idea with a variety of friends, colleagues and (of course) my "board" members. Two of the most helpful individuals are currently successful consultants; Dr. Chris Frings (Chris Frings and Associates, Birmingham, AL) and Ms. Debra Benton (Benton Management Resources, Fort Collins, CO). Chris and Debra shared their early experiences in launching their businesses and provided personal advice on avoiding some common start-up mistakes. It has been very helpful to have honest advice and feedback from Chris and Debra, both successful and experienced individuals.

CONTENTS

INTRODUCTION	1
CHAPTER 1 Timing IS everything: Your choice or theirs?	4
CHAPTER 2 Move up or move out? To stay or not to stay?	6
CHAPTER 3 Outplacement support: Don't leave your job without it	10
CHAPTER 4 Self assessment: Your skills, attitude and ability to add value	14
CHAPTER 5 The résumé: The introduction that speaks for itself, stands out and peaks the reader's curiosity	18
CHAPTER 6 Promoting yourself: The marketing campaign, target audience and tools to get there	23
CHAPTER 7 Networking: Love it or plan on a long vacation!	28

CHAPTER 8
Headhunters: The professionals that help you find
opportunities in the job market   34

CHAPTER 9
Electronic job searching: Finding your needle
in the vast array of haystacks   38

CHAPTER 10
The first phone call: Be prepared, be professional,
be honest and ask for the next step   43

CHAPTER 11
Interviewing: A two-way street, no need
to be nervous, you did your homework   47

CHAPTER 12
The employment offer: Think before you jump   51

CHAPTER 13
Alternative pathways: Take a different road or
try a new vehicle on the same road   54

CHAPTER 14
The beginning at the end: The successful end to your
search is the beginning of a new chapter in your career   58

CHAPTER 15
Thank you, I found a new home:
Don't forget to tell your new network of colleagues
where you are—keep in touch with them   61

CHAPTER 16
Resource list   63

INTRODUCTION

I have been an active member of AACC since 1974 and have served in numerous positions at both the local and national levels. In 1995, I served on the task force on the changing practice environment under the enthusiastic chairmanship of Dr. Lawrence Killingsworth. The task force was charged with a) examining the environment in which clinical chemists practice their profession; b) identifying trends and key drivers that most influence the practice environment; c) describing a best estimate for the future environment; and, d) listing professional qualifications necessary for clinical chemists to successfully practice in the new environment.

Most importantly, the task force was charged with recommending programs that would enable AACC members to practice successfully in the new environment. Then-president Dr. Mary Burritt presented the task force's recommendations in *Clinical Chemistry* in January 1996. After identifying core competencies in the areas of fundamental skills, clinical skills, scientific and technical skills, management skills, and professional development, the task force recommended that AACC create a Delta group to guide the association's efforts to create programs to help members achieve these competencies.

I remained active in the subsequent AACC committees and task forces dealing with helping members prepare for change. From my perspective, there have been two primary outcomes from these efforts. One is the evolution of the Delta project, which focuses on educational programs that help members develop the core competencies that the task force identified. The other outcome was the fact that various task forces successfully proposed changes designed to improve AACC's efficiency in presenting educational programs. I have the privilege of continuing with this effort as chair of AACC's newly formed distance learning group and as a continuing member of the Delta project.

This experience provided me with the opportunity to think about the rapid changes in healthcare and the associated industries — which for me meant the diagnostics industry. It also inspired me to stop and think about my own skills and marketability. Despite all of this experience preparing for change and assessing/updating my core competencies, there was still that chance that my skills would be incompatible with my employer's changing focus. Chance is a funny thing and change is constant in our industry. As luck would have it, I got a great chance (a.k.a. opportunity) to change and evolve even further. Fortunately, I was one of the lucky ones who worked for a good company with a people-oriented chief executive officer and I received good outplacement support.

Recognizing that not everyone employed in the laboratory medicine field is as fortunate, I was motivated to write this book. An overview of the process I went through, it focuses on helping readers find new positions in laboratory medicine and related fields. During my transition, I spoke with many peers and AACC colleagues and found that I wasn't the only one who didn't know that there was an entire industry available to help job hunters. My purpose is to make the reader aware of the concepts to consider before, during and after a transition period while providing more specific references for those areas one may want to explore in more depth.

The ideas presented here represent my experiences during transition and are not intended to be all inclusive. There are many ways to conduct a job search and you are encouraged to pursue your own ideas and a path that fits your specific situation.

Each chapter includes a closing section on "Food For Thought." These sections are intended to help you consider some of the less obvious concepts associated with each chapter. Before you begin, consider this…

FOOD FOR THOUGHT:

- Your value and identity are not based on your current job. Instead they are found in your self-esteem, personal life and overall career accomplishments.
- The difference between the impossible and the possible lies in your determination.
- A mind once stretched by a new idea, never regains its original dimensions. If your career is to evolve, you must keep stretching your mind.

Luck is opportunity meeting preparation.

Good Luck!

CHAPTER 1
Timing IS Everything: Your Choice or Theirs?

If you are reading this book, it is no surprise to you that the fields of healthcare and laboratory medicine are undergoing significant changes both in technology and in the operating policies being implemented by employers.

Anyone who has been through the exercise of "right sizing" in an effort to improve profits (even if you work for a non-profit organization) knows that this event can be quite the wake-up call. These days, if such an event catches you by surprise, you have been asleep at the steering wheel of your career and this book is intended to help you take control again.

My very first experience with outplacement occurred on my first full time job, some 20 years ago. It took the entire department by surprise. The corporation concluded that they had made a bad decision to enter into the pharmaceutical sector after less than two years in the business (it takes 7 to 10 years to bring a new therapeutic to the market). Our division's vice president got a call at home one evening to inform him that the entire department would be terminated the next day! This was before outplacement or severance packages were common and could have been quite devastating for everyone involved.

Fortunately, our vice president was vice president for good reason. His quick thinking, concern for people and good negotiating skills made the situation infinitely better than it could have been. He negotiated a transition period for the entire group, secretarial support for résumé preparation and a place to come to network (even before the term was used). He stayed until everyone in the group had a job and provided moral and professional support. The moral of this story? A corporation's decision may not be reversible but the way the process is handled says a lot about how much management values their employees.

The idea is for you to plan ahead and prepare yourself for a better position within your organization, find a similar position with another institution, or do something different that you really want to do with your life.

Don't wait until your employer tells you your services are no longer needed. Take time to assess your skills and determine if you can continue to contribute based on the directions the field is moving. Sometimes this planning process doesn't work according to your plan, which is why successful people are adaptable. Even if you are "The Person Successful Companies Fight To Keep" (Podesta 1997), your skill set simply may not match your organization's new plan. It may be time to acquire some new skills or change your approach to marketing your ability to add value to an organization.

The goal is that the decision to change jobs should be yours, not something that happens to you at an inopportune time. Once you make the decision, identify those individuals who will be of assistance and develop an implementation plan.

FOOD FOR THOUGHT:

- Receiving a severance notification at 4 p.m. on Friday can ruin your whole day (then again, maybe not).
- Losing a job is not the end of a career. It could be the start of a new one.
- Are your skills up to date and marketable?

CHAPTER 2
Move Up or Move Out?
To Stay or Not To Stay?

Changing jobs does not mean one must leave a good company or organization. If you have a record of accomplishments and fit the culture, there frequently will be opportunities to assume additional responsibilities or move into a different area of the company. On the other hand, if the policies and practices of your organization "drive you nuts" or conflict with your principles, it is probably time to move out. It is helpful to remember that chaos in the workplace (those times when the path forward is not clearly defined) can have advantages (if it doesn't take up permanent residence). Such times are opportunities for new leaders to emerge and test management's effectiveness when the road gets bumpy.

Moving Up?

Moving up cannot happen without support. Always start with your immediate manager. If an organization values employees, it will have procedures in place for career development planning. After checking with your manager, the human resources department should be helpful in explaining procedures. If you are lucky enough to be in such a situation, take this process with the utmost seriousness. Don't expect management to be serious about your career if you aren't. Take time to prepare for the discussion:

- Identify your career objectives and how they fit with the needs of the organization.

- List the accomplishments you have achieved in your current job and throughout your career.
- Identify your strengths and areas for improvement. Request the same information from your manager and compare notes.
- Develop a plan for moving up. Request the same information from your manager. Develop a mutually agreeable plan.

It is important that your expectations match those of your manager and the company. Work together to ensure that the plan has meaningful goals, opportunity to achieve the goals with management support (this often requires more initiative and commitment from the employee than the employer) and that progress is measurable in an objective way. If your objective is to move into another area of the company, always start with your immediate manager.

Should you be unfortunate enough to have a manager who is not interested in your career development, determine if this approach is limited to the manager or is widespread through the organization. If widespread, reconsider the "move-up" decision.

You may wish to develop a mentor relationship with a respected person in the organization if your manager is not helpful. Be careful not to create a difficult situation between your manager and mentor. Do seek advice from others in non-threatening ways. A good mentor will not speak poorly of your manager, nor will he or she allow you to do so. A mentoring relationship should have a positive focus and provide constructive/honest feedback and advice.

Regardless of the status of a career development process, make time to network within your organization. People who spend the entire day at their desks will have a great deal of difficulty knowing what is going on in the organization and what resources other people have that may help you, or them, do a better job. If you don't know what is coming down the road, your opportunities to proactively contribute are limited. I remember going through one down-sizing at a Fortune 100 company where the directors gathered together, were given a list of all the employees in the department, and told to list the five people they would like to have on their team. Those whose names appeared the most stayed; those who names appeared the least were given severance packages. This was clearly a case of "it's not what you know, it's who knows you."

Moving Out?

If "move out" is your decision, do not advertise this to your co-workers unless you are prepared to leave at a moment's notice. In some situations, it may be beneficial to discuss this decision with your manager or with human resources and ask for a "typical severance package." This frequently is successful, but be prepared in the event your request is denied. Never threaten to leave unless you are prepared to do so.

Whatever the conditions when you leave, remain professional and work with your employer to ensure a smooth transition. Make sure your records are up to date and all company property has been returned. When appropriate, leave a forwarding address. Ask to leave an auto-response e-mail message in your mailbox. The message should simply state that you are no longer with the company (so your contacts don't get returned undeliverable messages without knowing why). Consider leaving a home e-mail address in your message (but not your phone number…more on this later).

Staying on the Job While You Make Other Plans?

Sometimes you'll want to stay on the job while you make other plans. You might want to stay with the organization while you complete an educational program that will prepare you for a different or better position, for example. Or maybe you want to consider full-time consulting, but aren't ready to make the commitment right now.

In many cases, you can work with your employer to make these kinds of transitions successful. That's especially true in companies that offer voluntary separations as a way of reducing staff size. Be sure you understand your organization's policies and keep in mind the potential for conflicts of interest.

FOOD FOR THOUGHT:

- The field of laboratory medicine is a small world. Live your life such that if someone says something unkind about you, no one will believe it.

- Keep your bridges in good repair; good managers will be supportive long after you have moved to a new opportunity.

- Informal reference checks are commonly used. Don't think that the only people who may be contacted to find out more about you are those individuals you provided as references.
- In the current environment, the decision to "move out" may not be yours and may not allow you a lot of time for planning ahead.

CHAPTER 3
Outplacement Support: Don't Leave Your Job Without It

What is Outplacement Support?

Employers often provide outplacement support to employees whose services are no longer required as the result of some variation of restructuring. It is rare when leaving a position in "industry" that these services are not provided. In contrast, in the not-for-profit world, it is rare to receive such services. If your termination agreement does not include outplacement support, put this on the top of you list of benefits to ask for before you sign the termination papers.

So, what is outplacement support? There is a collection of local and national/international companies in the business of providing career counseling and support during a job search. You need not wait till unemployment (or as we say, transition) occurs to use their services. The services these organizations provide vary from basic to complete executive support based on the "package" you (or your former employer) have paid for. Some companies have internal career development centers which can be very helpful.

In all cases, the outplacement center provides a friendly, supportive place to go to. It's better than going to work each day since it maintains your routine but without all the hassles of your job. It does provide you with a whole set of new challenges in a supportive, coaching environment. With a personal outplacement counselor, you can understand and work through the various emotions related to grieving the loss of your job. Disbelief and anger are normal responses as long as you deal with them constructively and move your energies to developing your job search strategy.

> ***Remember that it's not what happens to you that is important. It's what you do with what happens that determines where you go from here.***

Take Your Time

It is generally recommended that you don't rush right into a job search effort. Take some time to collect your thoughts and address any issues on the home front first. Then you can focus on assessing your career plans, skills/accomplishments and develop a job search strategy.

Take advantage of the many (free) seminars held at the outplacement centers. These cover all aspects of the transition period from financial matters, to healthcare insurance, employment options, and all the aspects of the job search process. Start working with your counselor or reading the books recommended in Chapter 16. While you are developing and organizing your job search strategy, explain to those friends and colleagues who ask what you are going to do that you are using this time to assess your current status and formulate your plans. Thank them for their interest and let them know you will be in touch when you are better prepared to help them help you.

Outplacement/career development companies are experienced in helping you develop your career objective. This process includes an assessment of your personality traits (temperament), the type of environment in which you will likely succeed and a review of your previous accomplishments as background for the preparation of your résumé.

The personality assessment generally includes the Myers-Briggs Type Indicator (see resource list) along with a variety of other instruments and, depending on your package of services, may include an assessment by a qualified psychologist. The purpose of this part of the process is to provide you with insights and an understanding of the type and the characteristics of a new position where your skills and temperament will serve you and your new employer well.

Moving along in the process, one can now focus on the résumé. The format is fairly standard in terms of the content. The important part is not so much what you say, it's how you say it (more later).

Stop for a Moment to Make Sure You are Ready

Preparing the résumé is a significant milestone in the transition process. Everything up to this point is preparation for the formal search process. Your counselor will be a continuous coach during the search process, but before you begin your search, ask yourself the following questions:

- Do I have a positive attitude? Don't dwell on those negative feelings: you already put them to rest.
- How is my self-esteem? Your experience and new knowledge about yourself are excellent tools for this new adventure.

With your résumé in hand, the search process begins in earnest. Develop your marketing strategy and implement it with the same energy you would devote to any new and exciting project. The outplacement center will provide access to phones, typing/printing services, résumé mailing and a host of other services related to your job search, including market intelligence on the companies targeted in your search. Support for developing your interviewing skills varies from good advice to video rehearsal with trained interviewers and analysis after the interview (depending on your package of services).

Your counselor will provide objective help with negotiating a job offer and will keep in touch with you after you have accepted your ideal new position. Continue to cultivate this relationship. If you have been open with your counselor, he or she knows you quite well by the time you accept a new position and will be a good source for a "reality check" as new challenges arise in your new position.

JUST A NOTE: The outplacement world is not immune to mergers and other variations on restructuring. I was very fortunate to have received the executive outplacement package (with Millard Consulting Services, Fort Washington, PA) from Centocor Inc. following the divestiture of the diagnostics business. I met my counselor, Mr. Ed Kelleher, on the same Friday afternoon that my employment terminated. I worked with Ed for several months when the company he worked for was acquired by Manchester (an international outplacement organization). Ed started his own company, Kelleher Associates (Wayne, PA), and invited me to continue working with him

CHAPTER 3: OUTPLACEMENT SUPPORT

(which I was pleased to accept). Meanwhile, back at Millard, which became part of Manchester, I was introduced to a new counselor, Mr. Lee Curry, who I also worked with. The good news for me is that I have two counselors (both quite experienced but with different styles) and have experienced the philosophies of three different outplacement organizations. The process among the three organizations is very similar, but the specifics are different and the focus varies.

FOOD FOR THOUGHT:

- Searching for a job is a full time job in itself. An outplacement counselor can be a wealth of information on the process. Some also have contact networks they will share with you.
- Some employers provide for outplacement support because they care about their people (even their now former employees). Others provide for this service to keep legal activities to a minimum. Whatever the reason, outplacement support is a service worth bargaining for.

CHAPTER 4
Self Assessment: Your Skills, Attitude and Ability to Add Value

> *"You don't need to know a lot about people's weaknesses. But you need to know about their strengths. People gain confidence when you build on their strengths"*
>
> (Fast Company, November 1998)

Self assessment has many aspects and will vary with the stage of your career and the time you wish to commit to that career. This needs to be balanced with your family or personal commitments.

Getting Started

Perhaps the easiest way to start this process is to prepare a list of your job experiences and your education. Start with a simple list, then focus on selecting appropriate action words to describe your previous functions in a manner that describes contributions rather than just responsibility (more on this later). Keep this list close at hand as it will become the factual basis for your résumé.

Personality, Motivators and Objectives

Learning more about your personality traits and motivators will help you identify the types of environments that will help you succeed and the types of jobs that are likely to best utilize your strengths while minimizing your weakness.

A number of instruments ("tests") are available to help assess your interests (see resource list). Some common ones are:
- Strong Campbell Interest Inventory
- Jackson Vocational Interest Survey
- The Self-Directed Search

It is important that your interests are supported by your skills in order to be successful.

The most commonly used instrument for assessing personality/temperament is the Myers-Briggs Type Indicator. This tool defines four parameters and scores your preference toward opposite ends of each scale based on your responses to the questionnaire. The parameters are a) extraversion/introversion, b) sensing/intuition, c) thinking/feeling and d) judgement/perception. From these four parameters, sixteen personality types are described. This process has utility in understanding how different people (including yourself) are motivated, how they like to work and their preference for communication styles.

Skills

Your list of skills is derived from your experiences, but it is different. The application of your skills allows you to add value to a prospective employer. Understanding how to apply your skills to solve problems will serve you well during an interview when you are trying to convince a prospective employer that you are a better choice than other candidates with similar backgrounds.

As an example, you may be experienced in the techniques for processing biological samples for various laboratory tests (how to separate serum, how to store it, etc). From this experience, you probably became skilled in the concepts of pre-analytical variables and how these affect lab test results. This skill is applicable to preventing problems or problem solving in such situations as setting up outreach programs or regionalization of laboratory testing (where samples come from multiple sites).

Attitude

An objective evaluation of your attitude is a critical step in the self-assessment process. Attitude includes your outlook (optimist or pessimist, positive or negative) and the level of commitment you choose to give to your career relative to your personal commitments.

Optimism is a valuable trait. However, when carried to the extreme that one is unable to see potential problems (or challenges) or is unwilling to listen to "bad news," optimism can become a liability. Pessimism doesn't work very well unless inhibiting progress is a goal. Realism seems to be the balance needed for success. Always look for the good in situations and in people, but not to the exclusion of reality.

Only you can define your level of commitment to a career. There is "life after 5 p.m." so make sure that your career goals (and the accompanying time commitment) are consistent with the balance you set between work and home life.

Putting It All Together to Add Value

Completing this self-assessment process will give you an in-depth appreciation of your strengths and weaknesses and your goals for your job search. You will also discover that this process is a continuum and you will likely refine your goals (focus) as your job campaign progresses.

The best advice I received in my effort to "put it all together" came from Mr. Dave Holveck (CEO of Centocor, Inc). We met after I was displaced from Centocor to review my newly updated résumé and to talk about what I wanted to do next. Dave suggested that I look at my career up to this point from two perspectives and then relate the two.

- First, look at my career in blocks of 3–5 years and determine what I did and more importantly what I learned from the experiences in that period.
- Second, look at the events in the field during the same timeframes and determine what I learned from those events (were the events predictable?).
- Lastly, to put it all together, what would I have done differently if I knew then what I know now and what trends did I identify that might provide opportunities for my future?

(Note that this only works as a written exercise). Although this took about two weeks to complete (about twelve pages), it was a very informative experience for me. I review this document each time I prepare for an interview.

FOOD FOR THOUGHT:

- Although you may talk with a variety of people and use many different tools in this assessment, it is a self-assessment because the results are for your benefit. Be honest and take your time with the process.
- The better you know yourself, the more comfortable you will be during the interview process.
- With adequate financial and emotional support, your transition period can become an opportunity to seek out options you may not have previously had the time to consider.

CHAPTER 5
The Résumé: The Introduction That Speaks for Itself, Stands Out and Peaks the Reader's Curiosity

It's Monday morning in the human resources department following the company's advertisement in the Sunday employment opportunity section. Fourteen résumés have already arrived via fax, with another 23 by e-mail and 10 people have left voice mail messages inquiring about the job. Then there is the bunch that arrives by overnight express mail. Meanwhile, those contingency recruiters are busy calling their contacts to identify which résumés they can also send to join the collection.....and it's only Monday. Snail mail résumés will begin arriving tomorrow and for the next several days as the word gets out and the pool of job seekers compose their important cover letters, and those individuals that faxed their résumés earlier, will now send readable hard copies.

You have successfully made it through the very first step and your résumé has actually arrived on the desk of the correct person. But it is buried in that red file folder labeled position #CC4236 and you would like it to be noticed and acted upon…but how? I've not tried this, but you could use the birthday card approach (the ones that play music when you open them). It would be like when everyone in the lab got their new networked PC's where you selected a tune to notify you when a meeting was about to happen or you got an e-mail.

Seriously, there are several tips that will help your résumé get noticed.

Appearance

Getting noticed starts with a crisp, professional appearance. Your résumé will not get read if it looks like an amateur put it together.

The rule of thumb is that most readers spend less than 30 seconds scanning a résumé. Therefore, it is important to be clear and concise in the presentation. There are numerous books specifically dealing with how to write and format a résumé (see resource list) that should be consulted for detailed instructions.

Content

There are two basic types of résumés:
- Reverse chronological (lists experiences in chronological order starting with your current job)
- Functional (groups experiences by skills)

The reverse chronological is the generally expected type for scientific positions. The functional type may work well for non-scientific positions (or when changing careers), but usually raises a red flag when applying for scientific-related positions (both management and technical).

In the reverse chronological type, the format includes:
- Profile or career objective, which presents who you are and what you can contribute. This is the executive summary of your résumé and should provide all the relevant information absorbable in that 30-second scanning time.
- Work history/accomplishments that include a listing of each position held and a description of responsibilities and/or contributions
- Military experience (if applicable)
- Education, listing institutions attended and any special training (be clear on degrees earned vs. courses completed)
- Professional affiliations, honors, awards
- Publications, which should be on a separate page since you may not always want to include this section

Do not list your references on your résumé. Employers know that you will provide them upon request, so don't waste the space telling them. Also, a request for references will let you know that a potential employer has interest in your qualifications.

Length

Target your résumé to be one or two pages in length (excluding publications). A long work history may be difficult to fit on two pages, but the concept of concise still holds. Academic or government positions may be the exception to this advice. If you have been employed with an academic or government institution and your résumé is a small book, do not use this to apply for a position in industry (save it for later, but I don't believe that even a photographic memory can scan such books in 30 seconds).

> *SOME TIPS:*
> - Select paper and fonts that copy well. If you are selected for an interview, your résumé is circulated as a copy (maybe even a copy of a copy) and often is not readable by the time it gets to the interviewers.
> - Take a "top-down" approach to preparing your résumé. Consider what the new boss will be looking for (ability to solve problems and add value) rather than a "simple" list of accomplishments. "Put it together" for the reader.
> - The profile section should be sufficient to get noticed, present who you are and what you can contribute.
> - The body of the résumé should support the profile section and all facts should be verifiable. NEVER exaggerate or misrepresent your qualifications.
> - The résumé presents enough detail to interest the reader, but doesn't tell all. Leave something to talk about during the interview.
> - Always bring several original copies of your résumé to the interview and leave a copy with each interviewer at the completion of the discussion.

Now that you have your résumé and you are satisfied with it, take a little extra time to have it critiqued by professional associates who are in positions equivalent to the hiring managers you will be targeting. It may also be helpful to ask trusted peers to review it and comment on how well it represents your background.

CHAPTER 5: THE RESUME

Variations of Your Résumé

Depending on the level and type of search you are conducting, you may want to have several variations of your résumé. Each of these would focus on a different aspect of your background and would match the needs of the prospective employer you are targeting.

Electronic Résumés

The electronic résumé is an emerging concept. At this point, this mechanism is most used in the information technology field. If you apply for a position over the Internet, you will likely use an electronic version of your résumé.

There are some differences between "old-fashioned" résumés and electronic ones. Some employers use electronic formats for convenience (to save time or paperwork). In some cases, the résumés are electronically scanned based on key search words. If the search words do not appear in your résumé, you will not be further evaluated.

There is controversy about preparing a résumé in a "scannable" format. Résumés that contain bold or italic formats may not scan well and in some cases, may be rejected. In addition to the questions related to the format of the résumé for scanning, the concept of "key word search" is important. In essence, there are programs available that do the scanning. These vary in their level of "intelligence" and use of "fuzzy-logic." In some cases, words in the résumé need to be an exact match with the search terms. In other cases, "close enough" will work. The more sophisticated programs can "understand" what you are trying to convey based on a collection of terms used.

You can see the potential pitfalls in this process. Search firms frequently use electronic résumé scanning, but the larger more reputable firms (who you should be dealing with anyway) have the more sophisticated programs. This is an area to keep an eye on as this technology progresses and perhaps becomes more widespread in its application to scientific positions (especially where terminology and jargon abound).

The Cover Letter

Every résumé should be accompanied by a cover letter. In essence, this tells the reader who you are and what you are looking for in a new position. This is the primary mechanism to target your inquiry/application to a specific employer. It too needs to be clean, clear and concise. A cover letter longer than a single page is unlikely to be read.

FOOD FOR THOUGHT:

- A résumé is your introduction to the reader. You will not be present to explain or clarify it and your professional handshake and smile will not help (yet).
- I hope you would not interview wearing jeans and a T-shirt. Don't send your résumé "dressed" inappropriately.
- Your résumé should also leave a lasting impression after the interview. Leave a copy with each interviewer (at the end of the conversation). Remember that you are not the only person they are talking to and it is not always easy to keep straight which person matched which résumé. When the interviewing team begins to compare notes, it will be helpful to have your résumé in-hand should some question arise that was not discussed when you were there. If candidate 4 has some particular experience, no one may remember if candidate 6 (you) have the same experience.

CHAPTER 6
Promoting Yourself: The Marketing Campaign, Target Audiences and Tools To Get There

Many of life's failures are men who did not realize how close they were to success when they gave up.
Thomas Edison

Whether your target employer is an academic institution, a clinical laboratory or "industry," there are several ways to identify potential opportunities and different mechanisms to tap into these opportunities.

First a word on the "job market." Most job seekers spend their time searching in the so-called visible or formal market. However, there is an even more important and larger market, which is the so-called hidden or informal market.

The Visible Market

The visible market consists of any position that is advertised in a public fashion. These positions can be found in the want ads of various newspapers, on Internet sites like the ones in Chapter 9, in scientific journals or newsletters, through professional associations like AACC's employment exchange, through recruiters and even on the home pages of specific companies.

The problem with the visible market is that everyone else can find these jobs just as easily as you can and the competition is tough. Most outplacement professionals would agree that the visible market is a minor component comprising only about 25% of the total available market (the higher your level, the smaller the percentage of positions that are in the visible market). Note that even those positions in the hands of retained recruiters are generally considered part of the visible market (although perhaps somewhat less visible). By definition, the visible market consists of positions that are immediately available to be filled.

Approaching the visible market begins with you identifying a position you would like to apply for. Once identified, you will need to do some homework on the position and the company. It is always helpful if you have a friend or colleague at the company or institution that you can talk to about the position. (Perhaps it was your colleague who sent you a copy of a job positing in the first place). If the organization has a Web site, use it to identify the management team and the organization's products or services. Researching the management team will likely give you some insights on their areas of expertise (especially the technical individuals).

Try to identify what issues the company may be facing and formulate your cover letter (which always accompanies your résumé even if you send the résumé via the Internet) to demonstrate how your skills can be used to productively address those issues (i.e. "put it together" for the reader). Whenever possible, address your cover letter to a specific person (by name). Plan to follow-up on your letter by contacting the company. Note that this is not always possible and in some cases, the advertisement states "no calls." Demonstrate that you can follow any instructions that may appear in the advertisement. Always be sure your contact information is up to date and you are checking your messages frequently (the last thing you want is a frustrated potential employer because they can't reach you).

SOME TIPS ON ANSWERING EMPLOYMENT OPPORTUNITY ADS:
- Be selective in the ads you respond to. Don't waste your time if you are not really interested in the job.
- Always customize your cover letter for the specific position you are applying for.

- Address the requirements for the position and your relevant qualifications.
- Do not provide salary information in your cover letter. If this information is specifically asked for, give it careful consideration but remember that this is often used to rule in or rule out candidates (almost regardless of qualifications).
- Be careful with "blind" ads. If the position description looks particularly good (well suited to your interests), use your detective skills to make sure the position is not with your current employer or a partnering company of your employer.

The Hidden Market

The hidden (or informal) market consists of positions that may also be immediately available (but not yet advertised) or may be pending for a variety of reasons.

Some reasons that positions are in the hidden market are:

- An employee has resigned, creating an opening that has not yet been advertised.
- An organization is launching a new program and will need new employees.
- A particular program/project is working well and additional personnel will be added to keep it moving on schedule.
- An organization is about to achieve a milestone, such as winning a grant or receiving FDA approval, and will need additional staff.
- Perhaps a senior level person is about to retire and a replacement is needed or some other organizational changes will occur at that time.
- It might be the right time in the budget cycle when some pending positions are about to be funded.
- In some cases, positions can be created for an individual who has good credentials appropriate for the organization's needs.

Approaching the hidden market is a key element in your strategy. The concept here is networking (which you will learn more about in the next chapter) and there are many ways to network. The objective here is to be in touch with as many people as possible to increase your chances of being in the right place at the right time. You want those individuals who know of the pending positions to also know about you during (or before) the time that the position becomes available. Networking focuses more on telephone and face-to-face interactions than the written communications that are common (at least in the initial phases) to approaching the visible market.

The higher your level, the greater reliance you must place on your networking skills. All candidates should network (regardless of the job title you are seeking). In addition to the tools already mentioned, entry level individuals should utilize the employment centers at most universities, your professors and your previous employers (for any summer jobs or internships).

One of the most important and helpful tools in the networking process is the "information interview" (more on this later). In this situation, you are not seeking a job, rather you are seeking information and advice on your background and career objectives in the context of the field (laboratory medicine) in general. If you are prepared and ask good questions, this type of interaction (it can be a phone "interview" or a face-to-face meeting) is quite valuable in helping to reaffirm your objectives or make modifications based on the feedback/advice you receive.

Record Keeping

As you begin your search, remember to keep good notes and copies of all your correspondence. You will want to keep a list of each person or recruiter you have contacted, the companies you have sent your résumé to and an on-going log of the status of each contact. Be sure to record the phone and fax number in a readily available place. This may not seem very important initially, but as your list of contacts expands, you want to be absolutely sure that you know what you have already communicated to each contact (they will be at various stages in the process). Review your "file" on each contact person before making any follow-up calls or initiating the next level of communication. Keep the record close-at-hand in the event that the person calls you so you can scan the record while on the phone.

FOOD FOR THOUGHT:

- Remember that finding a new opportunity IS a full time job (and probably the only one you have right now). Plan to pursue your job search as a full time effort but remember that as with any full time job, there is time off for personal matters and vacation. You know what they say about all work and no play.
- Having a job search strategy and an implementation plan is no different than having a marketing plan for a new diagnostics product. In the clinical lab, it is the same as planning the introduction of a new analyte or service. How will you get people to know that the new product or service is available and how can you convince them that they want it?
- Keep an open mind during your campaign. Be willing to explore a new fork in the road that may not have been there when you started your search.

CHAPTER 7
Networking: Love It or Plan on a Long Vacation!

In chapter two, I illustrated a case of "it's not what you know but who knows you" when employees were being selected for termination. This concept works in reverse situations and is the basis for networking. When a position opens, you want to be the first person to jump into a potential employer's mind. Of course, you also want them to know you as a qualified person able to add value to his or her organization. If you don't have the skills to do the job, it doesn't matter much how many people know you. A good manager will not hire a "dud."

Stereotyping is not appropriate, but statistics can help to make a few points. Scientists and other technical people tend to have personality traits consistent with introversion (rather than the outgoing extraverts). Many scientists have difficulty speaking in public for this reason. If you fit the introvert category, you will need to pay special attention to the need to network, which will not come naturally for you. Use this time as an opportunity to overcome any resistance you may have to the idea. As the Nike slogan says, "Just Do It."

Starting a Network

As the process goes, you start networking with people you already know and expand from there (thus making it easier to get started). In the early days of my career, speaking to more than a very few people at the same time was something I was very much afraid of (I am one of those introvert scientific types). I got over it because I unintentionally put myself in a situation where I had to do it.

As an undergraduate student, I had an opportunity to student teach cell biology and physiology classes. I liked these classes, so I agreed and was very happy. Quite naively, I didn't think about the fact that I actually had to give lectures to a room full of people (writing the lectures was not the same as giving them). In fact, this did not occur to me until the first day of class when everyone had taken their seats and I found myself in front of the room (a bit beyond nervous). I will be eternally grateful to Carol and Steve, who were students in the class and also colleagues from my daytime job (we were all evening students). They happened to sit on opposite sides of the room and I lectured to each of their friendly faces, scanning the room as I alternated between them. By the end of the evening, I was actually looking at other people and I forgot about how nervous I was. The second class was so much easier and soon I actually looked forward to giving the lectures. I continued to teach these classes for eleven years (even after completing graduate school).

The moral of the story? Start networking with your friends and expand from there.

Your "Board of Directors"

One networking technique is to develop your own "board of directors" that can and will provide you with open constructive feedback as you develop and continue your campaign. The recommendation is that you have three to five board members during your search. These are individuals you respect and can go to for advice (at anytime). If you are just starting out, a professor or graduate school mentor may be helpful. As your career develops, you may find board members among your professional contacts (another example of why it is a good idea to actively participate in a professional organization) or your current/previous managers (a good reason to keep your "bridges" in good repair). Call your board members on a regular basis to keep them informed of your progress. They are good people to turn to when you are in a slump and need some encouragement, advice or just a good challenge.

The ABC List

The networking process is the most important part of your on-going job search (or campaign, as it is called). The whole objective is to tap into the hidden market by talking to many people (i.e. networking). Networking works best when the process is very systematic and organized. Before you begin, take time to organize your "story" and define your goals.

The process is sometimes referred to as your ABC list(s) or reverse pyramiding and consists of the following phases:

- Start by making a list of all the people you Already know (hence the "A" in the ABC list). These people are your friends (so they should be easy to talk to) and are the people you begin to network with. Talk to your neighbors, professional contacts from your work environment, individuals you met from your community and social activities, health professionals (doctors, pharmacists), financial and legal professionals, alumni association members, colleagues from professional associations and service professionals (hairdresser/barber, realtors, librarians, landscapers). In short, anyone of your friends or people you meet in your daily life who may have first-hand knowledge of the types of positions you are looking for OR anyone who may know someone who knows someone (you get the picture).

- People on your "A" list are the ones you are most comfortable talking to (like Steve and Carol on my first night of class). You may not think it is worth talking to all these people but it is a small world and you never know what will turn up. For example, my hairdresser has a client who works for a major pharmaceutical company and a person I met at an Alzheimer's support group (we both have relatives with this disease) has a neighbor in the healthcare field.

- The people on the "A" list will likely know someone that you can contact, thus creating a second list, the "B" (or Bridging) list. The B list will generally be larger than the A list since many people know more than one "appropriate" person.

- The B list will likely turn out to be multi-leveled, with a network of individuals bridging the way to the person who has the position and makes the hiring decision.

- The "B" contacts will, in turn, have a new set of contacts for you, bringing you closer to those individuals who Can hire you. This becomes your "C" list (completing the ABC list process).

As your network expands, it is easy to see how the inverted pyramid concept works (start small and expand). One nice part about this process is that the number of cold calls (to unknown people) is limited. The people on your B and C lists have all been referred to you through an initial friend on the A list. When you introduce yourself to a new contact, it will be easier because you now have a mutual friend or colleague (whose name you usually can use).

One of the less obvious benefits to this process is that when you do call your new contact with a referral from one of his/her colleagues, that gives you a higher level of credibility than a true cold caller would have. For example, if Dr. Smith tells you to call her colleague Dr. Jones, she wouldn't bother Dr. Jones if she thought you were a "dud." A note of caution, while you may start with a higher level of credibility, you need to be sure you are prepared for the conversation with Dr. Jones. The worst thing would be that Jones calls Smith to ask where she found this "dud" (now you have made a poor impression on two people).

Approaching People in Your Network

Now that you know how to find the people you want to network with, how are you going to approach them to obtain the information you need and what will you say? There is no single answer, but there are several options you should consider when gathering information.

- Depending on who the prospective contact person is, you may wish to contact him/her by phone or letter first, then follow-up with a letter or phone call. If you choose the phone for initial contact, you need to be prepared for the scenario that the individual does not answer his/her phone directly or does not take your call. Know before-hand what voice-mail message you will leave or what you will tell the assistant who answers the phone. If you are lucky you will get the desired individual on the first try (not a common occurrence). Give a very brief statement of why you are calling (including the name of the person who referred you) and ask if this is a convenient time or whether another time would work better (be sure to schedule the more

convenient time). Depending on how this plays out, you may want to send some written information about yourself as background for the follow-up conversation.
- Alternatively, you may wish to send a brief letter explaining your purpose and commenting that you will follow-up with a phone call.
- In general, your résumé is not sent during the initial contact phase. In some cases, it may be appropriate but be sure to comment that it is for information or background for the reader's convenience.

Regardless of which initial contact method you choose, there are several points to keep in mind.

- Remember that you are networking to receive information or advice. Your primary purpose is not to interview for a job. Remember you are tapping into the hidden market and these positions are likely not available yet. These kinds of interactions are commonly referred to as the information interview. Make it clear to the person you wish to talk to that you are not seeking a job, only their advice. This will take the pressure off the person you want to talk to and increase the likelihood that you will get the opportunity to talk. Remain true to your word about seeking information.
- The information interview can take place on the phone or face-to-face with the person (this depends on a number of factors, mostly beyond your control). Don't try to force one format or the other; go with your contact person's wishes.
- Be prepared for these "interviews." Before you begin, thank the individual for taking time to talk with you, then clearly and concisely state your objective for the discussion (i.e. looking for advice). Your primary purpose is to gain insights and advice on your career goals. Listen carefully and take notes.
- As with any interview, this is a discussion (not a lecture). Ask questions and respond to the other person's comments. Now is not the time to be aggressive; remember that you are asking for advice not competing against other candidates for a visible position.
- Thank the person again for their time and advice. Let him/her know how you plan to use the advice and what follow-up

actions you will take. Frequently, you will be given names of additional people to contact. Be sure to follow-up and keep the person you talked with informed of the outcome of your follow-up.
- Always send a written thank-you note regardless of the format of the interview.

The Value of Networking

Networking is indispensable to a successful job search and to keeping current on developments in the field. If you don't devote significant time to this process, you most likely will have an extended time in transition. If you fit the category of happy, currently employed individuals, you probably are not (or did not) paying much attention to developing a network. With the current status of the healthcare field, this can be a near fatal error in your career advancement. The time to develop a network is before you find your self in transition. The network I refer to is the total universe of people who may be helpful in identifying a new career opportunity (including recruiters) as well as those colleagues you can network with to keep up to date on the developments in the field (to help you keep your current job).

FOOD FOR THOUGHT:

- Once you adopt the process of networking you may be surprised at what you learn about the people and current events in your field.
- If you are sincere and professional in your approach, networking will restore your faith in humanity. I am impressed and gratified by the number of people who took time to talk with me and offer helpful suggestions.
- Sometimes you will run into a "dud." A comrade in the transition process related her experience of calling a "friend" who responded that he only talks to people who are employed. She crossed him off her list of friends.

CHAPTER 8
Headhunters: The Professionals That Help You Find Opportunities in the Job Market

Before you begin to work with recruiters, it is important to know how recruiters work. In general, the type of recruiter you deal with depends on your salary range. An extensive list of recruiting firms is updated annually in the Kennedy Directory of Executive Recruiters, found at many libraries and outplacement/career centers.

Take time to verify the recruiter's legitimacy before working with him/her. Never hesitate to terminate a relationship with a recruiter who is unprofessional or does not respect confidentiality. While in the negotiating phase with a company I very much wanted to work for, the recruiter told me (among other things) that I couldn't compare the offered salary to my salary at my last job because I was unemployed and therefore, my base pay was zero. He couldn't understand why I did not want him representing me during the negotiations! This is a case where the recruiter did a disservice to both the hiring company and the candidate.

If your salary range is above $75,000, the retained executive recruiter is for you. Individuals earning less than $50,000 generally work with contingency recruiters. As you would probably guess, the in-between folks are in between; some retained recruiters will work with candidates earning less than $75,000, but generally not less than $50,000. Contingency recruiters will attempt to work with candidates earning $100,000 or more.

Retained Recruiters

The retained recruiter is retained by a company to identify qualified candidates for a specific position. The only person working with the company, the recruiter seeks out qualified candidates, screens them against the company's requirements and "presents" several candidates to the hiring company. These recruiters are paid for identifying qualified individuals, whether or not any of the candidates accept the position.

Retained recruiters generally have developed long-term relationships with their client companies and are called upon when there is a hiring need. It is in the recruiter's best interest to identify quality candidates since they are not likely to be retained again if the candidate-turned-employee does not work out. For the candidate, this translates into a high probability of a viable opportunity if the screening process is successful. As a candidate, your objective is to have your name in the recruiter's database so when an opportunity does arise, you will be considered. Retained recruiters will not contact you unless they have an opportunity appropriate for your qualifications.

Contingency Recruiters

The contingency recruiter has a different operating process. They do not work for any particular company or candidate. Their objective is to find you a job because their compensation is based on a candidate accepting the job. As one contingency recruiter commented to me, he was "going to market the heck out of me." Thanks, but no thanks. My objective was to find the right job (not just any job). When I told him he could not forward my name without my prior consent, he never called again (just as well for me). Most contingency recruiters are very professional and the advantage of working with them can be their network for finding positions for which you may not have the right contacts to identify (until you get your networking skills in tip-top shape).

Employment Agencies

Sometimes known as job brokers, employment agencies generally work with jobs salaried at less than $40,000. They identify job openings through their networks and are compensated with a one-time commission when an employer hires a person they have referred.

There are several types of employment agencies based on the areas they focus on. The general type deals with a wide variety of fields. The single-industry type deals with a single field (e.g. computer specialists). The functional type specializes in a particular field (e.g. marketing or sales) which may be applicable to various industries.

Employment agencies may also be useful if you are looking for temporary employment. It is of interest to note that temporary work is no longer focused only on administrative support or entry level type jobs. Many firms are emerging that specialize in temporary management level positions. At this point, temporary management level positions appear to be limited in the scientific areas. However, using a technical background (and experience) for business development types of activities is growing especially as partnering, mergers and acquisitions continue to be the norm. Temporary employment keeps you active, provides a paycheck and often leads to full time employment. Such assignments provide an opportunity to test the "goodness of fit" between you and the employer.

SOME TIPS ON WORKING WITH EXECUTIVE RECRUITERS:

- Be prepared. Know what you want to do and the skills that qualify you to do it. Have your résumé ready and be sure the facts are verifiable.
- Be honest. Don't exaggerate your skills and NEVER misrepresent the truth.
- Be cooperative. Work with the recruiter to identify the appropriateness of a position. Don't say you are interested in a job if you really aren't. If you are not interested, consider suggesting someone else who has the appropriate qualifications (not just your buddy in the lab next door).
- Be professional. Return phone calls. Keep appointments.
- Be ready for rejection or success. Remember that the professional recruiter works to identify the candidate who best fits the position requirements. Be ready for the scenario where you are not selected for an interview. This is not a reflection on your ability to add value, rather a reflection on the goodness of fit.
- If you are successful in obtaining an interview, be prepared. Learn as much about the position and the company as you can. The recruiter will provide a written description of the position

and qualifications. Your network or the Internet can help you learn about the company.
- If you are working with a retained recruiter, don't bug them. Remember that they are working on specific positions. If your background looks appropriate, they will call you. The trick is to be in their database or even better, in their network. Once in the database, remember to keep the recruiter updated on any changes in your status or any significant new accomplishments.

FOOD FOR THOUGHT:

- The world of recruiters and search firms is one you should be connected to (even if you are currently employed). Develop a relationship with a few of the better recruiters you worked with.
- Remember that such a relationship is a two-way street. Help them keep your file up to date and use your network to help them identify potential candidates (as you work with recruiters who respect confidentiality).
- Never continue to work with an unprofessional recruiter. It is your career (and reputation), not theirs.

CHAPTER 9
Electronic Job Searching: Finding Your Needle in the Vast Array of Haystacks

I was the last person in my neighborhood to buy a microwave oven. Why would I need such a thing? Now I use it every day and can barely remember how to boil water for tea on the old-fashioned stove. The Internet was the same way. I resisted it for too long, but now, I use it every day.

The primary functions I use are e-mail, job-opportunity searching and intelligence gathering. There are numerous sites to help job seekers, but few are focused on biotechnology and healthcare. I have found several which are listed below. I have no connection to any of these and I present them for your information, which is not to be taken as a recommendation or endorsement.

I use some Web sites strictly for gathering information on what's new (the newswires) in the field. Others I use to see what's hot in the regulatory areas and some I use to track meetings and seminars of specific targets. Still others are focused on employment opportunities and you need to go elsewhere to do your intelligence work. Of course, there is crossover for many of these sites.

There are several places one can go to identify the ten to 50 best Web sites for job seekers. The problem with these lists is that few focus on healthcare and laboratory medicine. The following is a sample of such general Web sites. Some offer general advice on job searching and career development in addition to a listing of opportunities.

NOTE: All the Web site addresses listed here are proceeded by: http://

CHAPTER 9: ELECTRONIC JOB SEARCHING

General Career Web Sites *(NOT NECESSARILY RELATED TO HEALTHCARE)*

www.careercity.com	Career City Cutting Edge Careers
www.careerbuilder.com	CareerBuilder Network
www.careermag.com	CareerMagazine
www.careermosaic.com	CareerMosaic
www.careerpath.com	CareerPath.com
www.collegegrad.com	College Grad Job Hunter
www.cweb.com	CareerWeb
www.dice.com	DICE (high technology jobs)
www.excite.com/careers	Excite careers network
www.futurestep.com	Korn/Ferry and Wall Street Journal career page
www.iccweb.com	Internet Career Connection
www.jobtrak.com	JOBTRAK (university centers)
www.monster.com	Online career center
www.selectjobs.com	Jobs for computer specialists

Healthcare Career-Focused Web Sites

www.biocareer.com	Biotechnology career center
www.medhunters.com	Job opportunities for healthcare professionals
www.medsearch.com	Career resource designed specifically for healthcare professionals
www.medzilla.com	Healthcare related jobs, résumé posting and job search related articles

Healthcare-Focused Web Sites

Note that some sites are free, while others have subscription costs for all or part of the site.

www.bio.com	Biology related corporate and academic positions
www.BioSpace.com	A comprehensive biotechnology site
www.bioworld.com	Biotechnology information and job bank

www.cato.com/biotech	A virtual library and career center for biotechnology
www.globalmanagedcare.com	Global managed care issues
www.healthrespubs.com	Healthcare industry news and intelligence
www.hin.com	Healthcare Intelligence Network: information on the business of healthcare
www.medscape.com	Includes "Journal Scan," a clinician's guide to articles in current medical literature; features clinically-focused summaries of articles addressing topics likely to impact clinical practice
www.sciweb.com	Life science resource and career center

Company or Institution Homepages

Company or institution homepages are great sources of information about both the company and employment opportunities. You have developed a list of target companies for your job search. Try entering *www.companyname.com* and see if they have a homepage. More often than not this works. Sometimes it gets more tricky when they use initials or abbreviations. Most biotech and pharmaceutical companies have employment sections on their homepages and you can apply for a specific position via the Internet (if your résumé is transmittable). By the way, you may want to send your résumé to some friends, with different word processing programs, over the Internet to be sure it comes out the other end in a readable format.

The same concept holds true for most major educational institutions. Try entering *www.institutionname.edu*. For academic positions, try www.academploy.com for the academic employment network or chronicle.com/jobs/ for the Chronicle of Higher Education Career Network.

CHAPTER 9: ELECTRONIC JOB SEARCHING

Organizations (i.e. the ."org" sites)

These are great sources for intelligence, updates and/or job opportunities.

www.aacc.org	American Association for Clinical Chemistry
www.ama-assn.org	American Medical Association (JAMA on-line)
www.bio.org	Biotechnology Industry Organization
www.diahome.org	Drug Information Association
www.jcaho.org	Joint Commission on Accreditation of Healthcare Organizations
www.nejm.org	New England Journal of Medicine
www.who.int	World Health Organization

Government Sites for Intelligence, Some Employment Opportunities and Regulatory Updates

www.ahcpr.gov	Agency for Health Care Policy and Research
www.cdc.gov	Center for Disease Control and Prevention
www.fda.gov/cdrh	Center for Device and Radiological Health
www.fda.gov	Food and Drug Administration (lots of options within this site)
www.fedworld.gov/jobs	Listing of all federal jobs
www.HCFA.gov	Health Care Finance Administration
www.ncbi.nlm.nih.gov	National Center for Biotechnology Information
www.sec.gov/edgarhp.htm	Securities and Exchange Commission (annual reports and other financial filings for publicly held companies)
www.uspto.gov	U.S. Patent and Trademark Office

News Wires That Have a Healthcare/Biotechnology Section

www.prnewswire.com
www.businesswire.com
www.reutershealth.com

Newspapers/Magazines

Several on-line newspapers and magazines will allow you to set up a job search strategy using their want ads. You select the criteria and they search for you. If an opportunity arises, they e-mail you (if you selected that option) to notify you of the opportunity. I have done this with Business Week, but to date did not turn up any suitable opportunities. I think the types of jobs I am looking for are just not in this magazine (but it was interesting to get the biweekly updates of related information I should look at). So this is a great service depending on your field of interest. By the way, this is a free service and you don't have to subscribe to the magazine.

FOOD FOR THOUGHT:

- The Internet will become a valuable tool in your job search. If you are not already adept at using it, make this a priority for your professional development. The Internet is an excellent way to keep up to date on the current developments in the field. This information is necessary to remain competent in your current position as well as to identify new opportunities.
- If you are not already on-line, practice your networking skills and find a colleague who will help you. You will also find a host of courses offered through adult education programs. If you are a dedicated introvert, buy some books and teach yourself.

CHAPTER 10
The First Phone Call: Be Prepared, Be Professional, Be Honest and Ask for the Next Step

There are two types of phone calls you need to be prepared for. The ones you place and the ones you receive in response to your letters or other inquiries.

Calls You Make

Although you will probably be sending out many letters and résumés, you may want to make some initial contacts by phone.

When you do, there are some points to keep in mind.

- More often than not, you will reach an assistant. Explain who you are and your purpose for the call. Ask to speak with the individual you are calling. If he or she isn't available, inquire about a convenient time for you to call back (this keeps you in control of the ongoing conversations). Ask to schedule some time on the person's calendar.
- When you do connect with the individual, confirm that the time is convenient. This is a bit risky but is the considerate thing to do. Thank the individual for taking time to talk to you.
- Concisely state your purpose for the call and comment on any previous exchange of information that may have occurred.
- If you have been referred to this person by a colleague, be sure to state that at the beginning of the conversation.
- Do your homework on the individual and the company and

have your list of questions ready. Be prepared to listen (without interrupting).
- As the discussion nears a close, ask about future actions. Can you get together for a more detailed discussion? Should you send any additional information? Are there possible opportunities you can follow-up on?
- Close the call with a thank you and statement of any actions that you will take as a result of the call.
- Be sure to follow-up on your commitments.

You will not always be successful in reaching a contact by phone. This is just reality and should not be taken personally (but do give it some thought if it happens with every contact). It will take some persistence, professionalism and a little luck. Most executive assistants are very helpful and will make you feel more at ease. Consider that a good executive would not keep a grumpy assistant as it is a reflection on the executive. In any case, you need to always be professional and pleasant (if you are in a grumpy mood, call a real friend or take a walk, but do get over it).

Calls You Receive

The most exciting calls are the ones that come to you while minding your own job-search business. Most of your contacts will not call just to say hello (although, your friends might). So when the phone rings, be prepared. Answer in a pleasant professional voice. It could be a recruiter or hiring manager with the perfect job or it could be someone selling you vinyl siding for your apartment in a brick building.

Assume it is a call for a potential interview:
- Keep a pen and paper near every phone you use (especially if you get the call at home).
- Be upbeat for these calls. The caller can "hear" more that you may realize in your voice.
- Have your résumé in front of you so you can clarify any questions the caller may have. This will also help you remember exactly what you presented in the résumé and when you completed each accomplishment.
- Be prepared to discuss your career objectives and your executive summary of your background. This is often called

CHAPTER 10: THE FIRST PHONE CALL   45

> your 90-second commercial (that's about all the time you get to introduce yourself and present your most notable skills/accomplishments).

- Above all, be honest in answering any questions. A "positive spin" is anticipated but don't exaggerate; you may get in trouble later.
- Work with the caller to set up an interview in a timely manner. If you already have a golf game or afternoon high tea scheduled with friends for that day, I would go with the interview.
- Reconfirm the specifics of what you agreed to (date, time, place). If the outcome of the call was not an interview, try to determine what the next step in the process would be.
- If the call was to convey an end to this particular path, ask the caller if he or she has any advice for you to help with your search or to change some aspect of your presentation style or content. (This may help identify and prevent some "mistake" you may have made during the interactions related to this particular opportunity.)

Of Course, the Best Call to Receive Is the One with an Offer of Employment

This topic is covered in more detail in Chapter 12. At this point, it is important to mention that the tips listed above still apply. Be professional—you can do your little joyous dance when you hang up the phone. Never accept a job over the phone. Tell the caller you are "encouraged" (or some such sentiment) and would like a written offer and some time to consider the offer. Agree on a reasonable time to think about the offer before responding (you may have other opportunities in the works that you need to weigh and may want to accelerate that process if that is a better opportunity). You will need the offer in writing to be sure all the details are as you understood them from the verbal offer you received. After reviewing the offer letter, plan the conversation for when you place the return call to negotiate the terms of the offer.

In Summary

In short, the phone is a rapid way to contact people in your network. The success of this approach will depend on your skills and the willingness (or availability) of the person you wish to make contact with.

Whenever possible and geographically feasible) consider a face-to-face meeting (even if it is only 30 minutes and it takes one and a half hours to drive there). I was fortunate enough to have a face-to-face information interview with a well-respected physician and director of a major department at a university some 50 miles from my home. I initially had some reservation that the 30 minutes allowed for the meeting may not be productive. My concern was unfounded and it turned out to be one of the most productive and informative "interviews" I have experienced.

FOOD FOR THOUGHT:

- In this era of electronic communication, a face-to-face meeting or a phone contact is more memorable. To some individuals, talking has a greater impact and is more memorable than the impersonal e-mail communication.
- Always give consideration to the preferences of the individual you wish to contact. A potential advantage to e-mail is that the message can be read anytime of the day and a very busy person may prefer that method of communication. The disadvantage is that there is no opportunity to discuss a particular point and in some cases your intention is left to the reader to deduce from the printed word without the benefit of the inflections in your voice.

CHAPTER 11
Interviewing: A Two-Way Street, No Need To Be Nervous, You Did Your Homework

> *You never get a second chance to make a good first impression.*
> John Malloy

There are numerous good books on the specifics of interviewing, so I will not go into that level of detail here. See Chapter 16 for some suggestions.

It would be simplistic to discuss the types of interviews you are likely to encounter. There appear to be as many styles/formats as there are people interviewing. Perhaps the most difficult is when the interviewer is not prepared or is inexperienced with the process. These can be the most difficult for you to get your message across. If you both are unprepared, the conversation may focus on fishing or shopping but not on the job, so you both lose the opportunity to learn about each other.

Interviews can take place in a variety of settings: over the telephone (common initial format), in hotel rooms (a colleague experienced this and it was indeed an odd process), restaurants, someone's office, someone's home (over dinner with the family), a conference room with one or several people, and may include a formal presentation. In all cases, you need to be prepared by knowing yourself and being a good listener as well as a good speaker.

Points to Consider Before the Interview

- Do your homework on the company and yourself. Prepare your list of questions you would like to cover during the interview. It may be helpful to review the many available books suggested in Chapter 16 that offer answers to interview questions.
- Give some thought to your appearance. Dress up for the occasion (I mean the traditional business suit) even if the organization is casual. Get dressed the night before to make sure a "stitch in time" isn't needed since the last time you wore the outfit.
- Know where you are going and how long it takes during the time of day you have the interview. A dry run beforehand is a good idea, but remember it will generally take less time at 8 p.m. than at 8 a.m.
- Be sure to write down the phone number of your contact person and bring it with you.
- By all means arrive on time (this means 10 to 15 minutes before your scheduled interview). If some awful thing happens on the way, make sure you can call your host and let him/her know. Better yet, leave enough time to anticipate such traffic delays (if your transportation is provided, this is a bit more difficult).
- Use the few extra minutes to visit the restroom and comb your windblown hair and check for stray poppy seeds detracting from your smile. Talk with the receptionist; he or she usually has a way of making you feel welcome and comfortable.

Points to Consider During the Interview

- You have done your homework so there is no reason to be nervous. Remember that if the interviewer didn't already see something positive about you, you would not be there for the interview. Ed Kelleher (one of my outplacement counselors) explained it to me in terms of the interviewer being the host and I, the guest. It is rare that a host (or hostess) will be rude or inconsiderate to their guest. If they are, there is a message there!
- An interview is a two-way street. It should be a conversation, not a trial by the judge. Both of you are there to gain information about the other to assess how well you and the company fit together. In my interviewing experience, the

inexperienced interviewers haven't read the books on interviewing and experienced interviewers have a different set of questions. The basic questions on your background and what you want to do are common (but you are ready for them from your self assessments and preparing your résumé and career goals).

- Remember to have professional presence, as explained by Debra Benton (1992) in Lions Don't Need to Roar.
- Bring enough clean original copies of your résumé to give to each interviewer as you conclude the discussion with them. They probably already have a copy, but not an original of your masterpiece.
- Have a discussion with your interviewers. Avoid one or two word answers. Use their questions to help you promote your talents and value to the company. Choose some of your answers so that they lead into a question for the interviewer.
- Of course, never be rude or inconsiderate to your host or hostess (be they the interviewer, their assistant or the receptionist).
- At the conclusion of the interview, ask for feedback. Also ask about the next step in the process and the timeframe for it to happen.

Points to Consider After the Interview

- As soon as possible, sit down and make some notes. How did you really answer those questions? Are there any you would have answered differently or in more detail if it wasn't such a surprise question? How did you feel that the interviewers responded to you?
- Write a thank-you note to each interviewer. Don't send the same letter to all of them; personalize it based on the focus of each conversation.
- If you do not get some feedback in a reasonable amount of time (you will need to define reasonable), initiate a follow-up call. Balance being persistent with being a pest.
- If this particular opportunity does not work out for you, try to get some feedback. Was it just not a good match? Or, was there something about your presentation that made a poor impression? Seek this information carefully and in a non-

threatening manner. The information you get back can be very valuable as you continue in your campaign.

FOOD FOR THOUGHT:

- Always consider an interview as an exchange of information. Many of the current interviewing literature recommends that you should focus on "selling" yourself. While this is good advice, it is critical to understand the "selling" process. A person skilled in the art of selling knows that understanding the customer's needs is the crucial first step. It would indeed be unfortunate if a multi-talented candidate promoted the "wrong" skills to the interviewer because he/she didn't take time to understand the interviewer's needs.
- Another important aspect of "selling" is the need to develop rapport with the prospective buyer. Remember that it is a natural tendency for a manager to hire a person he or she "likes." Engage in purposeful conversation during the interview.

CHAPTER 12
The Employment Offer: Think Before You Jump

*If you don't know where you are going,
any road will take you there.*

By the time you get to this stage, you have invested a lot of time and energy in defining your career objectives and the type of new position you were looking to find. It has been an adventure getting to this point and now you have the first formal offer of employment. Should you accept it? Sure is tempting and you are ready to end this transition stuff.

Well, think about it before you accept. You set your goals and know what kind of environment best fits your personality/temperament. Does this job fit your criteria? If you were careful with the companies you interviewed with, the offer letter will likely describe a position close to your expectations in an environment compatible with your personality.

If so, it is time to negotiate the specifics.

Getting an Offer

Initial job offers typically come over the phone. Do not accept a job offer over the phone based on an initial conversation. Tell the caller that you are encouraged by the verbal offer and ask for a written offer. A written offer ensures that you understand the details—it is possible that in your excitement you may miss some important points of a verbal offer.

Thinking It Through

Review the terms of the offer letter. Decide which items are the most important to you and rank these items in order of your priorities ("must have," "nice but not critical" and the little extra "icing on the cake"). Evaluate each of the items to determine if the specifics are acceptable. For example, if salary is your number one "must have" priority, is the $50,000 offered close enough to the $52,000 you need? If not, can it be negotiated to a higher level? Maybe there is some other benefit that compensates for the difference? Look at your transportation costs. Is this job closer to your home or can you avoid the tolls to make up the $2,000? It is helpful to know what salaries and benefits other organizations in the field are offering.

The point here is to look carefully at the offer. The total package should be considered, not just as it appears on the surface. If any item falls short, is it worth turning down the offer? Perhaps it depends on where on your priority list the item falls.

After you have carefully reviewed the offer (remember to consult your board members, your counselor and significant other). Make your list of issues to negotiate, however large or small as they may be. There will always be some items to negotiate (if you don't think so, you are missing an opportunity). Remember the time to negotiate is before you accept the offer. It is too late once you sign on the signature line.

Negotiating

When it is time to call the company and let them know your response, the following tips may help:

- Be prepared for a counter-proposal or a substitution of some other benefit for the one you are looking for. For example, a "joining bonus" may substitute for a higher salary that cannot be offered (for equity reasons).
- Maybe keeping your three weeks vacation (as opposed to the usual two weeks for starting employees) is important to you. Ask for this if it is not offered. Note that if you move from an academic institution to industry, you may experience a

significant decrease in vacation and holiday time (in my case, I went from almost five weeks to two weeks...that was tough but the new position was worth the sacrifice).
- Perhaps reimbursement for education is important to you. This can be a significant chunk of money that you don't have to put out of your pocket if you are planning to continue your education. Inquire about support for professional association membership.
- Sometimes, medical benefits can be used as a bargaining tool. If your spouse has a policy that covers you, it may not be necessary for you to have the benefit also. Some companies will compensate for this, others will not. It never hurts to ask.

It helps to be knowledgeable of salary surveys and the types of benefits offered by organizations like the one you are negotiating with. The tools you can negotiate with depend on your level and the type of environment you are moving into.

Don't be shy, but don't be unreasonable either.

FOOD FOR THOUGHT:
- Your financial and personal situation may have a significant influence on the time available to find a job (not to mention the right job). Receiving an employment offer is a happy event especially if your time in transition has been longer than you thought it would be. In the long term, it is likely to be a big mistake to take a job you will not be happy with (just because it was offered).
- The time to negotiate the employment conditions is before you accept the job. Remember that these interactions result in the development of a business agreement. Approach it as you would any other business agreement/contract. Be professional, positive, and open and look for the "win-win" agreement.
- You have worked hard to get to this point. Don't miss the opportunity to celebrate with those who have been supportive and worked with you during your transition.

CHAPTER 13

Alternative Pathways: Take A Different Road or Try A New Vehicle on the Same Road

The message here is don't get stuck in a rut. As Dr. Chris Frings says, "If you always do what you always did, you will always get what you always got" or the Dr. Lawrence Killingsworth version "If you only do what you always did, you will get left behind!"

Back in the early stages of your transition process, you spent significant time on self assessment. During that time, you probably considered different career alternatives. Maybe your campaign focused on one of those alternatives. But maybe you decided to seek a position similar to your last engagement. Keep in mind that the world of employment opportunities continues to evolve, especially in the sciences, and "new" fields emerge. Frequently, your skills are transferable to another field and enhancing your current skills often can take you into an emerging field

Here Are Some Examples of Alternative Pathways

- An alternative (recommendation during the outplacement process) for one of my employees was to consider teaching junior or high school biology. While neither he nor I would have thought of it, in retrospect, I could see him being very good in such an endeavor.

- Another colleague with a technical marketing background decided to try his hand at the world of finance and landed an offer.
- Another of my employees, a medical technologist by training, transferred to the pharmaceutical side of the business in the data management area for clinical trials. Her familiarity with medical terminology and the significance of lab test results are an asset for her and she has expanded her horizons and marketability in a new area.
- A colleague with expertise in regulatory affairs had begun a program at a local university to obtain his law degree. This combination of a technical/scientific background and a legal background is a good route to go if you have the right temperament. Many are successful along this road.

Consider applying your technical skills to the world of information management. It seems that every day there is a new Web site providing medical/technical information to both clinicians and patients. The managers of these sites need individuals skilled in various aspects of healthcare delivery.

Consider some emerging areas such as genetic counseling, pharmacogenomics, alternate-site testing and outreach programs, integrated medical infomatics, drug discovery and delivery technology, clinical studies and outcomes research, medical writing to support product/drug introductions (when was the last time you read a clear, useful package insert?) or perhaps teaching in a non-traditional setting.

Then There Are Those Who Pursued or Contemplated a Career Change

- One clever long-term employee asked for a severance package (and got it). He used his time off to enroll in courses at Longwood Gardens towards becoming a master gardener/landscaper.
- Another employee is evaluating opportunities in the culinary area. Perhaps something he enjoys and does well will turn into a rewarding career opportunity.

As I commented earlier, changing jobs does not necessarily mean changing employers.

While with Johnson & Johnson, I held various positions, each with different technical responsibilities. At various times I participated in or managed the development of RIA's, EIA's (manual and automated), reagents and instruments for flow cytometry and single-test assays for physician offices. The point here is that I had the opportunity to broaden my technical expertise not only in various technologies but also in different medical/clinical areas. Remember that your skills are transferable.

Another colleague, still with J&J, has broadened her expertise from the area of product development, to include both quality assurance and marketing. In her case, the medical area remained consistent, but the aspects of the business she learned has grown and expanded.

A colleague at Centocor, with many years of product development experience, moved into the project management area (while with the same company). Upon the divestiture of the diagnostics division, she found a position in project management with a major pharmaceutical company. In her case, she moved internally, which served as a stepping stone to a new (but related) career (i.e. project management) in a new environment (i.e. pharmaceuticals).

Consider Making Your Own Road

In all the examples above (except maybe one—the jury is still out), these individuals remained employed in "traditional' settings working for an employer with an anticipated steady paycheck. Of course, there is the option of becoming self-employed, perhaps a much more daring approach.

There is much to be said for being your own boss. You will never again have a bad boss. (At least I hope so!). But there are two sides to every story. It also isn't easy being the boss (and maybe everyone else in the company too). The ins and outs of entrepreneurialism are beyond the scope of this book. But thinking about this option is certainly a worthwhile exercise and a viable option for many individuals. Perhaps one particular type of entrepreneurialism, consulting, may be right for you.

Perhaps You Have a Small Fortune and Enjoy Risk and Pressure

How about the world of start-up companies and venture capital? If you don't want to start your own company, there are lots of good (or maybe not so good) ideas looking to become reality. Perhaps you may fund these endeavors for a percentage of the potential profits. Perhaps you may join a start-up company in its early stages of development. This is a risky business, but the rewards (personal and financial) can be great. This is not for the faint hearted or the casual personalities.

How About Retirement?

Retirement just isn't what it used to be. Not many folks take to the rocking chair these days (although it is not a bad way to pass time if you have a suitable porch on which to watch the world go by or chat with the neighbors…what an old-fashioned idea! If your finances are in good order, this may be one of the options to consider.

These days, retirement is an opportunity to step out of the rat race and try something you really like to do. Perhaps it's strictly recreational, or spending more time with the family. Perhaps you might want to start your own business; you certainly have lots of wisdom and experience by this time in your life. You might consider teaching at a local college (if that fits your personality and communication skills).

FOOD FOR THOUGHT:

- Many people (myself included) who have gone through the outplacement process say it is an experience everyone should have (just once). If you (can) take advantage of the time and self-assessment process, it is an opportunity to ask yourself what you would like to do rather than keep doing the same thing because there is no time to think about anything else.
- In some cases, losing a job can be a wake-up call to take charge of your career.
- If you like what you do, don't change for the sake of change. Focus your energies on keeping your skills up to date as the field continues to evolve and new skills are continuously needed.

CHAPTER 14
The Beginning at the End: The Successful End to Your Search is the Beginning of a New Chapter in Your Career

It has been a long road. Sometimes it seemed like it would never end. But it did and now you have to adjust to your new environment. It is a new beginning and you are prepared for it. The time you invested learning about yourself early in the self-assessment process should be put to good use now.

If you relocated your home and/or family during the process, you will need to maintain a balance between the needs of the new job and getting settled at home. This will be a hectic time, but a positive approach (the same one you have become accustomed to during your search) will set the tone for how things go at home. If it is an adventure, the children (and significant other, a.k.a. spouse) can have fun too and go through the same process that you are emerged in on the job. You all will be learning about the new environment and making new friends.

On the job you will need to scope out the terrain. Identify a few individuals you will be interacting with and spend some time with them to help you understand the new corporate culture. Don't develop that bad habit of staying at your desk all day. Go to lunch with several colleagues and ask questions about how things work in the organization and how the boss likes to conduct business. Remember back when you were doing the Myers-Brigg personality traits you learned that different types of people need to interact in different ways.

With time, you will develop a good understanding of what you are expected to contribute and what your role is within the department and company. What you actually do should be compared with the job description you received. Ideally, reality and theory should match. If you don't have job description, develop one with your manager. There is some debate about the need for a job description and its value/hindrance in promoting creativity. This may be appropriate in some fields, but most scientific positions still fit within the old school of thought and use job descriptions. If others in your group or company have one, make sure you do also.

Focus your activities on the priorities of the department while developing a list of accomplishments significant enough to show your real potential and value. Don't simply complete lots of "little" things to create a long list.

As time goes on, don't assume you are doing a great job. You will need to develop a good rapport with your manager and make sure you are meeting his/her expectations. Ask for feedback in a formal way (it could take a few minutes or you may want to have a real meeting). How you get this feedback depends on how your manager likes to interact. Regardless of the mechanism, be sure to get the feedback you need.

It will be helpful to formally meet with your manager in a three- to six-month time frame to get some formal feedback and discuss any issues you may have identified. This is a good time to discuss short- and long-term priorities and implementation plans.

Soon, you will be an old timer with the company. The networking skills you developed during your search continue well into the adjustment period in your new environment and everything is going well. Your new colleagues have accepted you and respect your skills and contributions. Your new manager is pleased with your performance and has given you added responsibilities (and compensation).

While all of this is good, it is important that you not fall asleep at the wheel of your career. Keep your technical and management skills well tuned. Periodically review your self-assessment and career objectives. Update these as your situation changes and your career continues to evolve. Keep your network outside the company up to date. This will help you to keep current on the events occurring in the field and help others keep you in mind when yet another great career opportunity arises.

FOOD FOR THOUGHT:

- A new job is a great opportunity to make changes in your image or mode of operating. One director I worked for was a California native, quite intelligent, very competent, highly respected and a bit of a non-conformist. His attire was neat but casual. Everyone knew when something "important" was going on because that was the only time this person wore a suit. In contrast, his peers and the "higher-ups" always wore the traditional corporate suit. In retrospect, such "non-conformity" didn't exactly help that individual's career. Upon taking a new job at another company, this director "dressed the part" and no one at the new company gave it a second thought.
- Don't lose sight of your new/revised understanding of yourself gained through the self-assessment process.
- Enjoy your new adventure and maintain a balance among the various aspects of your life (e.g. job, family, professional development, recreation time)

CHAPTER 15
Thank You, I Found A New Home:
Don't Forget to Tell Your New Network of Colleagues Where You Are— Keep In Touch With Them

Congratulations! Your campaign has been a success and you have found a position to meet your objectives and give you room to grow and contribute to a new employer. As I said before, this is the beginning of your new adventure and another chapter in you career.

During the process of getting here, you made many new friends and developed a network of professional contacts. The worst mistake you can make now is to forget about all those people that helped you.

You should send out what is called the landing letter. Let all your contacts know where you finally landed and how they can get in touch with you in your new environment. This is a simple one-page letter containing all the pertinent information (what you are doing and how you can be reached) about your new job and may include your new business card (if you have one).

Those individuals who were especially helpful may be pleased to be your guest for lunch or dinner. If distance does not lend itself to dining, some other gesture of appreciation would be appropriate.

As time moves on, it is important to keep in touch with your network of friends and new colleagues. Call them from time to time, send them some interesting piece of information (an article on a topic of interest), or just call to say hello.

The closing line on the CD ROM I received (and used) from Ed Kelleher while at Millard Consulting states:

To Have A Friend, Be A Friend

How true!

CHAPTER 16
Resource List

A collection of books for general career or personal development and job search-related activities.

Books

Adams (1999) Electronic Job Search Almanac 1999, Adams Media Corporation, MA. Note: This publishing company has a extensive series of career and job search related books. The "JobBank Series" lists jobs by geographic region, state or large city. (A complete list of publications can be found at www.jobbank@adamsonline.com)

Araoz, D.L., Sutton, W.S., (1994) Reengineering Yourself: A Blueprint for Personal Success in the New Corporate Culture, Bob Adams, Inc Publishers, MA.

Barrett, J. and Williams, G., (1990) Test Your Own Job Aptitude, Penguin Books, NY.

Beatty, R., (1996) 175 High Impact Cover Letters (2nd Edition), John Wiley & Sons, NY.

Beatty, R., (1998) The Five minute Interview (2nd Edition), John Wiley & Sons, NY.

Benton, D.A. (1992) Lions Don't Need To Roar (Using Leadership Power of Professional Presence to Stand Out, Fit In And Move Ahead), Warner Books, NY.

Benton, D.A., (1996) How To Think Like A CEO: The 22 Vital Traits You Need to Be the Person at the Top, Warner Books, NY.

Block, J.A. and Betrus M., (1997) 101 Best Résumés, McGraw Hill, NY.

Blohowiak, D., (1995) How's All The Work Going To Get Done? How to Manage the Challenges of Churning Our More Work with Less Staff, Career Press, NJ.

Bolles, R., (1999) What Color is Your Parachute: A Practical Manual for Job-Hunters and Career Changes, Ten Speed Press, CA.

Boufis, C. and Olsen, V., (1997) On The Market: Surviving The Academic Job Search, Riverhead Books, NY.

Covey, SR., (1989) The 7 Habits of Highly Effective People: Powerful Lessons in Personal Change, A Fireside Book (Simon & Schuster), NY.

DeLuca, M., (1996) Best Answers to the 201 Most Frequently Asked Interview Questions, McGraw Hill, NY.

Fine, J., (1997) Opportunities in Teaching Careers, VGM Career Horizons (a Division of NTC Publishing Company), Linconwood, IL.

Fry, R., (1994) 101 Great Answers to the Toughest Interview Questions (2nd edition), Career Press, NJ.

Gale, L., (1998) Discover What You're Best At: A Complete Career System That Lets You Test Your Own True Career Abilities (Revised for the 21st Century), Fireside Press, NY.

Hamilton, L., (1999) WOW! Résumés for Health Careers: How To Put Together a Winning Résumé, McGraw Hill, NY.

Hancock, C., (1998) Health Care Career Starter: Finding and Getting a Great Job (includes a Directory of Training Programs and Financial Resources), Learning Express, NY.

Hansen, K. and Hansen, R., (1995) Dynamic Cover Letters, Ten Speed Press.

Hirsch, AS., (1999) National Business Employment Weekly Interviewing, John Wiley & Sons, NY.

CHAPTER 16: REFERENCES

Hunt, C. and Scallion, S., (1999) Navigating Your Career: 21 of America's Leading Headhunters Tel You How It's Done, Wiley & Sons, NY.

Kennedy Directory of Executive Recruiters (yearly publication), Kennedy Publications, NH.

Korea, O. and These J., (1988) Type Talk: The 16 Personality Types That Determine How We Live, Love & Work, Dell Publishing, NY.

Logue, C.H., (1993), Outplace Yourself: Secrets of an Executive Outplacement Counselor, Bob Adams, Inc Publishers, MA.

O'Connor, L., (1999) Ten Top Dumb Career Mistakes and How To Avoid Them, VGM Career Horizons.

Podesta, C. and Gatz, J., (1997) How To Be The Person Successful Companies Fight To Keep, Fireside, NY.

Swanson, B., (1995) VGM Professional Career Series: Careers in Health Care, VGM Career Horizons.

Tieger, P.D. and Barron-Tieger, B., (1995) Discover the Perfect Career for You Through the Secret of Personality Types, Little Brown and Co., NY.

Tieger, P.D. and Barron-Tieger, B., (1998) The Art of Speed Reading People: Harness The Power of Personality Type and Create What You Want in Business and Life, Little Brown & Company, NY.

Yager, N. and Hough, L., (1998) Power Interviews: Job-Winning Tactics from Fortune 500 Recruiters, John Wiley & Sons, NY.

Yate, M., (1999) Knock 'Em Dead, Bob Adams, Inc Publishers, MA.

Yate, M., (1998) Résumés that Knock 'Em Dead, Bob Adams, Inc Publishers, MA.

Newspapers/Magazines

National Business Employment Weekly
For subscription information: PO Box 300, Princeton, NJ 98543; 1-800-JOB-HUNT.
 Weekly articles on all aspects of job searching, frequently with lists, quizzes and references

Fast Company
For subscription information: PO Box 52760, Bolder, CO 80321-2760
Monthly publication with articles on the work environment (www.fastcompany.com)

Other Tools

Executive Advisor (Self Directed Career Management) (1996)
A CD ROM from Career Interactive, Fort Washington, PA 19034
Takes the observer through the process of a career search with sample résumés and letters for various purposes.